Tip Book for Direct Sales Leaders

Written By

Victoria Sheffield

100 Tips for Direct Sales Leaders is Copyrighted by Victoria Sheffield 2018©. This book was published by Jeru Publications. www.jerupublications.com To order extra copies email me at sheffieldvictoria39@gmail.com—Feel free to follow Business Coach Victoria Sheffield on facebook. There you will also find my web address.

Introduction

Many take the huge step in starting a direct sales business. There are some that seem to think that direct sales is pretty much the same as pyramid schemes. Little that they know about this billionaire industry. The truth is that many people in this type of business are very successful. I know because for the last 17 years, I've enjoyed working with one of the top direct sales companies. (Avon) When I started my business I made up my mind that I would succeed no matter what.

I've joined a few companies over the years and became very successful with the others too. What I now know is that most direct sales companies operate pretty much the same. With proper training and support anyone willing can be successful. Other things that can help is having great products and services to promote. A positive attitude, hard work, and a consistent system can make the world of difference. In this book I hope to share with direct sales leaders simple things that can help with prospecting, growing a strong team, and making sales.

Tip #1

If you sell products, keep a few with you at all times. I keep a small travel case in my car filled with at least 20 products. If your company is service based, keep business cards and brochures on you at all times. Always be ready to do business no matter where you are.

Tip #2

Stay Positive! Even when things look impossible your attitude can play a huge part in your success. Believe, work hard, & be patient. In other words don't give up on your business. You will reap the benefits of your hard work soon enough.

Tip #3

Be Professional! Call clients and prospects back asap. Keep appointments and make sure you offer the best customer service around. How about sending first time clients a thankyou card after they use your services.

Tip #4

When doing vendor or networking events, make sure you're prepared. Take plenty enough business cards, samples, brochures, etc...This is not the time to be shy........So kick the shy habit! Meet and greet new people. Pass out business cards and talk to as many people as you can. Greet them with a friendly smile and don't forget to take an email list with you. Don't forget to ask them for a business card as well.

Tip #5

Do you have a company journal? If not visit a dollar store and pick up one. Write down a list of people that have mentioned to you that they are interested in what you have to offer. Try writing down people that either do not have a job or people that could use extra income. Try to get two forms of contact information then share your success.

Tip #6

There is power in text messaging!

Try texting your contacts this. Hey I have something I want to share with you. When they respond arrange a time to talk with them and share your new business with them. Make sure you are ready for any questions. If contacts do not wish to talk or are too busy to talk, try texting them a link to your website with a message. A great message could be I am sorry it's been hard reaching out to you but here's my website so you can see what I've been up to. If a person shows no interest or does not respond I would not send a second message.

Tip #7

Here are a few tips for social media marketing. Try adding a clickable link when posting ads and flyers. I know from experience that adding this link will help increase website visits. Check your website analytics. This will show you how many people are visiting your website. You can also check this on your social media platforms. Analytics can even tell you where traffic is coming from. This way you'll know which marketing efforts are working the best. So do your research and read up on this subject.

Tip #8

Try not to look at your business as if you are selling anything. Of course you know you're into sales but think of it as sharing opportunities. Try not to appear to be selling anything at all. At the right time, share what you feel prospects need. Your company has great products or services that will sell themselves.

Tip #9

Write down everything! When you hear clients mention that they are interested in certain things, jot it down in a notebook. If you sell products write down a list of products and supplies that you may want to add to your inventory. Write down new ideas about ways to market your business. Then read over your notes twice weekly.

Tip #10

If you are on Twitter, you can link your facebook page. This way your tweets will automatically be posted on your facebook page. This saves you time when you're marketing on social media. Remember to interact on social media and add new friends.

Tip #11

Post before and after photos. Do this to show people proven results. This could work with services as well as products. Try charting the progress of clients when using services. If you sell weight loss products, hair products, etc...you could post photos to show that the products work.

Tip #12

Leave business cards everywhere. When people ask you for your phone number automatically give them a business card. Give them to your children's school teachers. Place them on billboards. Give them to waiters, tellers, and anyone you come in contact with.

Tip #13

Make sample packs — Sample packs are very small baggies made of business cards, flyers or postcards, samples, coupons, or just anything that you would want potential clients to have. Ziplock bags are really good for this. They can be small or large baggies. Kick this up a notch and add a few mints and ribbon.

Tip #14

Kill the poor sales pitches. People can tell if a sales person is giving them a sales pitch. Think of creative pitches that will help you generate sales. Chances are if you've heard it before then most of us have too. Here's a great pitch. One of the reasons why I love what I do is because I enjoy helping people change their lives for the better.

Tip #15

Market even while on vacation. We all need a break but a great direct sales leader is always working. Even if you are in a different state you can leave flyers, sample packs, and business cards with people you meet.

Leave them in restrooms, hotels, and at car rental places.

Tip #16

Here are a few ideas for places to leave marketing materials. Leave them: laundry rooms — doctor's offices — grocery store buggies — taped on apartment mail boxes — hospital lobbies — bulletin boards — work break rooms — teacher's lounge — bus stops — corner stores — gas stations donut shops — car mechanic shop — dressing rooms — bank tellers shoe stores — temporary staff offices — unemployment office

Tip #17

Go to as many sales meetings as you can. The meetings are very helpful because direct sales leaders can learn from others that are very successful. This can be very helpful in understanding that high goals can be achieved. Your company may even offer webinars or conference calls. Use every opportunity to learn.

Tip #18

Try using lead boxes. They can be ordered or you can be creative and make your own. They come in handy at networking and vendor events. They can even be helpful if your company does home shows. When doing free give-aways leads can put their personal information on a form or questionnaire you've provided.

Tip #19

Learn to listen to what people need. People will tell you exactly how you should approach them if you would just listen and observe. Take it all in and be ready to refer the best products or services according to what they need. Be willing and ready to change lives.

Tip #20

Don't ever measure up to someone else's success. Once you set realistic goals that work, put forth every effort to make your goals work. It takes time to build any business. Sometimes we are on the outside looking in on someone's success without knowing what they had to go through to get there.

Tip #21

Follow Up With Clients. Whether people are potential clients or people that do business with you, always follow up with them. When people purchase products or utilize your services, always reach out to them and find out if they are satisfied with what they received. If people have inquired but haven't done any business yet, follow up with them anyway. Sometimes people have great intentions but forget to call. Some could be waiting on you to call.

Tip #22

Do all of your sales training. Each company has their own method of training but make sure initially when you join a company that you take advantage of learning everything you know about the business. Read over everything and don't feel ashamed about asking questions.

Tip #23

Wear company t-shirts, hats, buttons, etc...Someone is bound to ask questions about your company. Remember to invest in you. Be creative and go the extra mile that it takes to market and grow your business.

Tip #24

Start a blog! Many business owners are blogging to help boost sales. Even if you are a person inexperienced in this area, you can learn. Blog about new products, special updates, sales, and services offered. If you are totally clueless in this area, search the web for blogs that cater to what you do and take pointers.

Tip #25

Be consistent! If you put very little time into your business, you will get very little back in return. If you consistently work your business, you will reap the benefits of your labor. Working on a business one week and skipping the next just won't cut it. Neither will one day a week.

Tip #26

Build relationships — Get to know your clients. Listen to them and find out what they need and want. Show them that you are a genuine person that is concerned about their well being. People purchase things from people they like and trust.

Tip #27

Be teachable — Learn from others mistakes. Your mentors have been there and done that so to speak. Any great sales leader can tell you that they have tried just about everything. They usually know what works and know what it a waste of time. Even if you are a person that is a little apprehensive, listen and learn.

Tip #28

Meet new clients in an open public place. Safety first means everything. Only do parties through referrals from people you know. We all want to succeed but being careful and safe is a plus.

Tip #29

Use a financial planner. Balancing and budgeting will play a huge role in your success. Knowing where every penny goes and how much money is received will help determine how much money is earned. Try creating one yourself if you're really good with computers or search the web for free ones.

Tip #30

Try tossing brochures. I will admit that I haven't done a lot of this but I know people that do. What's tossing? Tossing is bagging up your brochures, business cards, samples etc... and tossing them on lawns. Some toss a lot of baggies and some only toss what is left over from events or parties. I would not suggest doing this on a day when rain is in the forecast. Remember to never open anyone's mailbox.

Tip #31

If you are a person that does not have many people in your circle, start going to more social events. Visit Eventbrite at eventbrite.com to find events in your area. Some of the events are even free. My only advice would be to choose those events that you have carefully researched. Try searching the event host on facebook. Check to see if there is a website.

Tip #32

On brochures, business cards, and flyers, always leave more than one contact method. This way just in case people can not reach you for any reason they can always email or text you.

Tip #33

Let people know that they are free to text you. Some wonder if this is ok. Rule of thumb, I always let clients know that they can text or email me at any time of the day or night. If you only want clients to call within certain hours make sure that you note this on flyers and all of your marketing materials.

Tip #34

It is very hard to become a top seller by yourself. Get helpers! These are people that can refer clients to you. You can reward them with money or by giving them free products or services. Make sure that you offer them a special coupon code or a special way to track their referrals. Helpers may also be great people to recruit on your team.

Tip #35

Always be creative! Think of new ways to market your business. Get a journal and write down unique ways to build what you do. Remember that there are many doing the same thing as you. Try to think of ways to make your business stand out in the crowd. Observe what others are doing and stay a step ahead.

Tip #36

Develop a system that works for you. The old saying "if it isn't broke don't fix it is true." This system can always be tweeked but stick with the plan. Trying new things is perfectly fine but if you are successful with what you are already doing keep up the good work.

Tip #37

Personally I enjoy speaking with at least 3 a people day but if direct sales leaders are to climb the ladder of success, then increase the numbers. If three or less is comfortable then stay there but if you can squeeze in another surely your numbers will grow. Try to gradually build your business.

Tip #38

We all want the big pie in the sky. If your sales volume sky rocked today, are you ready? Ask yourself this because I've been there. I prayed and prayed for more. When it happened I started receiving a large volume of emails not to mention the messages to answer on social media. Then there are the large volume of phone calls to answer. So think about how you will handle the success.

Tip #39

Make boss moves! You're a business owner and making decisions that may cost you is not the thing to do. Make smart decisions that will impact your business for years to come. Many have great potential but do not carefully think about ideas and promotional campaigns.

Tip #40

If the person that recruited you is not the best leader or barely reaches out to you, please do not allow this to define your success. We just can not blame others for our level of success. There are great mentors to follow in every direct sales company that I've been apart of. Follow these people on social media. If they create training videos on Youtube subscribe to their channel and make sure that your post notifications are on. To learn more about that do a search on Google.

Tip #41

Market your business on the radio. Some of the online platforms offer budget friendly rates as low as $10 believe it or not. Shows can list your business as a sponsor plus you can even go live and do an interview. For example I have a broadcast that does advertising and social media blast starting at $10 and up to $25. Search facebook for the CWBN Network International.

Tip #42

Wake up everyday speaking positive affirmations. Here are a few examples of speaking positivity in your life. Today I will put forth my every effort in working my business. Even though the numbers are not where I want them to be, I know that in time change is coming. I am predestined to succeed. It feels great to be able to work my passion. Speak life into your business. Negative thoughts and words will determine the success of a business.

Speak Them and Believe Them!

Tip #43

Don't feel responsible for the failure of a recruit. Your job is to recruit and train to the best of your knowledge. Recruits can only show team members how to be successful. We can't make them do the work.

Some will come and some will go but keep on focusing on building a strong team.

Tip #44

When team members or recruits are doing really well reward them. This will motivate them to even better. Incentives don't have to be expensive. I've even known some to give cash rewards. Most companies have really great compensation plans but if you are someone interested in building a strong team you may want to consider personally rewarding your team.

Tip #45

If you are into sales leadership and building a strong team, build yours first. Great leaders lead by way of example. When your team sees your success, they will want to succeed also. They will even reinvent the wheel in most cases and follow your lead.

Tip #46

Knowing how to talk to clients on a professional level is a plus. If you are someone that uses profanity, it wouldn't be wise to use it while talking to clients. Gossip and speaking down on your company should never be done. Speak clearly and use professionalism at all times.

Tip #47

Be Yourself! Many try to be successful by mimicking what others do. Work on being the best you by being unique. What works for one person may or may not work for the next. It's perfectly fine to get ideas from people especially if a person is learning but remember that you were created with your own style.

Tip #48

Show clients your company's guarantee. Many would much rather do business if they know that they would have satisfaction guaranteed. For example if clients purchase products will they be able to return them if they don't like the products?

Tip #49

Create Presentations: Are you into powerpoints or creating videos? When meeting clients they can be used to help clients or prospects understand certain key points about your company. Some companies even have their own presentations.

Tip #50

Close your sale: Do this as soon as you notice that your potential client wants to order products or use services. Simply ask them if you can go ahead and write their contract, process their invoice, etc... This can also be done with recruits. After you've explained terms, ask them if this is something that they agree with or if they are ready to start their new business.

Tip #51

Learn how to create landing pages to promote your business. A landing page is a call-to-action page with one goal. The goal depends upon the marketer. For example a page may be created for those interested in natural health. The page title may be "Learn How to Heal Your Body Naturally". There may be a sign-up sheet, a link to a website, or even a video to watch. To learn more research how to create landing pages.

Tip #52

Work on personal development. What can you do to better yourself as a business person? Work on communication skills. Work on professionalism. Work on the areas that you feel need improvements. Learn everything you can about direct sales, marketing, and lead generation.

Tip #53

Be willing to go all the way out. Don't think that bold marketing efforts are too over the top. Don't be afraid to go all the way out for something that you believe in. Draw attention, gain exposure, and never stop promoting.

Tip #54

Try using paid traffic on social media. Google AdWords and facebook advertising are two ways to boost traffic. These are also cost effective ways to market. Advertise as much or as little and use target marketing to grow your fan base.

Tip #55

Create a monthly marketing budget. For example each month I automatically take $50.00 of my earnings to put back into my business. What you put into a business is what you will get out of a business. Try to think long term. Fifty dollars spent today can earn hundreds of dollars and even more in the future.

Tip #56

Try asking customers for referrals. Let clients know that if they pass out your business cards, brochures, or literature etc... that you will give them a free gift or a certain percentage off of their next order. Reward them for their time. Chances are they will recommend repeat referrals.

Tip #57

Become a guest blogger. Search the internet for people that have blogs in your niche area. How about sending them a message and asking them if they are in need of a guest blogger. Most bloggers will allow guest bloggers to add their website details. This works well with blogs that have a large amount of followers.

Tip #58

Be Useful! Ask yourself how can you help the community with what you do. Do you have something that you can donate to shelters or the less fortunate? Use this as an opportunity to share your information with facility owners or managers.

Tip #59

Get people to write product or service reviews for you. Ask them if you can post their review on your website. Reviews can also be posted on social media. A great tip is to get them to post reviews on your social media pages themselves. The only flip side to this is that they should be your pleased clients.

Tip #60

Do product or service reviews. This would means that you'd need to use the services or products that you offer yourself. This way you can share honest reviews. If you are a blogger, you can create a blog specifically for reviews. Some are even creating video reviews which may be more convincing.

Tip #61

Volunteer to help out at events. This way you can meet new people. Volunteers usually receive free tickets. This is another opportunity to pass out business cards. Try joining networking groups on facebook for your town.

Tip #62

If you are good at speaking, volunteer to speak at events. If you volunteer your time free, you may be permitted to sell your products or services. A way to find speaking opportunities is to type speakers wanted or needed then whatever your town is in facebook's search area.

Tip #63

Build a foundation of trust. Make commitments with clients and keep them. Give your honest opinions and make sure that you are loyal. Do great work. Be the best at what you do. This way your clients will trust that they are getting the best service that you can offer.

Tip #64

Make a great first impression. The first time you meet or call a client, make sure you operate in a professional manner. This just may determine if the client will use your services again. Smile, make eye contact, and thank them for doing business with you.

Tip #65

Make sure you honor your companies guarantee. For example if your company guarantees satisfaction then make sure your clients are happy. This may mean processing returns on products or working with a client that is not happy. Understand that in most case scenario the customer is always right is helpful.

Tip #66

Try to work with clients that are on a budget. Does your company offer products or services for people on a low budget? If a person specifically states that they are on one be ready to recommend only what they like and can afford. When your company has special promotions try notifying those clients.

Tip #67

Make sure you understand your companies compensation plan. For example before you join any direct sales company make sure you understand what percentage you will be earning from sales. This would be a question that the recruiter can answer. This will alleviate joining a company and not being happy with earnings. Some companies offer low percentages which can depend on many factors.

Tip #68

Always have a plan B. Do direct sales companies go out of business? Yes they do! Has this ever happened to me personally? Unfortunately yes it has. Carefully research companies and consider those that have been in business a long time. Don't be afraid to try new things.

Tip #69

Try not to allow life to slow you down. Life happens and always will. Think about it like this. If you were or are working a job it would be difficult not to clock in every being faced with troubles. We that are in direct sales must clock in even when we do not feel like it. In other words being self employed is not a license to work if and when we feel like it.

Tip #70

Market your business on Snapchat. There are some believe it or not that are successfully marketing their business on there. Search Google for how to market a business on Snapchat. Entrepreneurs must not be afraid to try something different. You may just be surprised.

Tip #71

Do what you are telling your team to do. In others words, don't be a hypocrite! It's not do as I say you should do. The message should be that leaders should lead by way of example. I'd feel pretty bad sharing advice with my team members knowing that I've never tried what I am telling them to. The best way to know if something works is to try it yourself.

Tip #72

We've all gone through it! Do you feel yourself slacking or just not pushing yourself to market your business as much as you use to do? Be true to yourself and find out if you're still passionate about what you do. Sometimes life happens but If so, pick up the pieces and get back in the game.

Tip #73

Have an online party for your team. Facebook is a great place for doing online parties. If you have team members, you can create one flyer for all of them to share on social media. This way team members can invite friends from their guest list. The flyer should read: (online party and the date) Free give-away to the first person that attends. Remember give-aways should be very cost effective. Try giving away services or samples.

Tip #74

Take pride in what you do! Work your business with a spirit of excellence! In other words strive towards perfection and rock your direct sales business. This will determine the outcome of your success.

Tip #75

Make Appointments - Take the time to schedule appointments for meeting or speaking with clients. This may help with calling clients at times that may not be good for them. This will also give direct sales representatives time to create a presentation catered specifically to client's needs.

Tip #76

Create a system for staying in touch with clients. For example once a month I email each client to let them know about new items or special promotions. Following through with this will help with staying on task. A system may include a phone call or even a text message. Everyone has a different system but having one makes things easier.

Tip #77

Just because you have a team does not mean that you can not learn from them. Learn from them and take their ideas to grow your entire team. One hand compliments the other. So humble yourself down and allow each team member to share ideas. You could even add your own flavor to their ideas.

Tip #78

When you see team members doing a great job let them know. This will motivate them to do greater things. I've even shared my teams accomplishments on social media to let the world know how proud I am. Motivate and encourage them to try new things.

Tip #79

Do you market on social media? People LOVE freebies. How about writing a very short ebook and giving it away for free. The ultimate goal is to get people to visit your website. So don't forget to include your web address in the ebook and in your social media post.

Tip #80

Grow your email list. Make sure that you are adding new people to your email list. If there are people that do not wish to receive emails, quickly remove them. One way to avoid this is to ask them if they mind you sending them emails.

Tip #81

Work on sales techniques. Take a look at everything you are doing to see what's working. If some of your efforts are not working, don't be afraid of change. The things that are working, try using those techniques more. One way to find out is by paying close attention to the numbers and by documenting everything you do.

Tip #82

When clients do not use your services or order products, do not take this personal. Who knows why this happens. Perhaps they loss a job or can not fit this into their budget. Try calling them up to see if they are ok. A great conversation starter is hi there I haven't heard from you in a while. I just wanted to see how you're doing.

Tip #83

Give your kids business cards to take to school. If they are a little apprehensive, reward them. Make sure that they tell their friends to give their parents your business cards. If you have a company that has samples, they can even give samples to friends to give to their parents. If you make a sale, pay them a buck. They'll be motivated to help you more.

Tip #84

Become a part of the welcome committee in your neighborhood. You can give gifts to new neighbors. Try making an inexpensive gift basket with a welcome letter in it. Purchase supplies from your favorite dollar store. You can even use recycled supplies from holidays. Exchange numbers if you can. This way you can follow up to see if they enjoyed their gift basket.

Tip #85

Host a ladies night out! This way you can network and share your opportunity, services, or products with your guest. If you can not find vendor events that are within your budget, create your own events. Restaurants are a great place to do this.

Tip #86

Start a lay-away service. This could work out for those that do not have the money to pay in full. Make sure that they understand all of the terms. Your guidelines may be that within 30 days they would need to pay in full.

Tip #87

Don't be afraid to ask people if you can set up a table at their event. This may be a small or large table. Even if there are no products to sell, informational tables help people to be informed about what it is that you do. Some will even allow business owners to do this even if they are not offering vendor spaces. Storefronts are another place to inquire.

Tip #88

Don't toss your old business cards, flyers, postcards etc... A penny saved is a penny earned. If your phone number, email or web address has changed, use small labels to cover up the old information. The new information could even be put on the back of your marketing materials.

Tip #89

Does your company offer services in bilingual format? If so, market to the Spanish community. Think about how much business you could be missing just because you're leaving them out. It wouldn't hurt to learn how to speak Spanish.

Tip #90

Barter services! You can even barter and trade products with other business owners. Maybe they have something that you need. This could save money if you're smart. Remember only to barter if you REALLY need what they have to offer. This could work out well at vendor events. Sometimes vendors purchase from vendors.

Tip #91

When team members decide that they want to join another company or stop selling, don't get discouraged. Let this be the driving thing to motivate you to work harder. Not every company is for everyone. Not everyone will work as hard as you.

Tip #92

Find out what your team members goals are. Some wish to only earn a few extra dollars and some want to make a full time career out of what they are doing. These are usually the ones that will work harder. Learn how to work with team members according to their specific goals.

Tip #93

Put forth your best effort in training all team members regardless of their goals. Just because a person has small goals does not mean that some time in the future they won't have larger goals. Some change their mind and decide to increase their goals.

Tip #94

Never under estimate team members. Just because their sales volume is currently low now does not mean that in the future they won't work harder. Some join companies and do well from the beginning. Some people take much longer to understand what it will take to be successful. Your job as a recruiter it to be supportive and to provide mentorship when they need it.

Tip #95

Invite people to weekly team meetings or calls. This way they'll get a chance to hear tips from other successful people in the business. They can also get a feel of what it would be like to join your team. Sometimes being able to experience the support system will help determine if they want to join.

Tip #96

Work together as a team! No team can be successful by being jealous or envious of one another. Celebrate each others success and create a supportive environment for team members. This will motivate them to recruit others to join. They'll also enjoy participating in group trainings sessions.

Tip #97

Have an event to launch your business. People do it all the time when they write books. Why not do this so that family and friends can see what you're doing? Your upline can even help out with this event. This can be done in your home or on a larger scale.

Tip #98

If the only time you have to work on your business is one hour day, use that hour wisely. You can get a lot accomplished in one hour. Maybe you are working another job. You can use your hour to send out emails, to follow up with potential clients, to market your business, and to create an effective marketing plan.

Tip # 99

Show work at home moms how to grow a business from home. Many choose to become stay-at-home moms but do not know how to balance it all. You can teach moms how to do this by showing them how to work their business in between diaper changes, kids naps, etc...

Tip #100

Create a facebook group for your clients. Have them post a photo of their purchases in that group. If they are using your services, have them to post testimonials in that group. Direct sales leaders can even play games and be creative to keep clients interested in the group. Make sure you stay active in the group by posting new items or services. How about giving them a free gift or service after posting so many times? Remember give-aways don't have to cost much money.

Bonus Tip #1

Show your team how to grow their business using social media. This means that you will need to use social media to leverage your own business. Direct sales marketing plans are duplicable. When they see you marketing on social media, they can follow your lead.

Bonus Tip #2

Show people your companies success! People would much rather join a company that they know is successful. Post accomplishments on social media. Use accomplishments during presentations.

Bonus Tip #3

Try not to over market yourself on your personal facebook page. Use a business page to post in daily. You can post as many ads as you want on your facebook business page. Posting too many sales ads or pitches on your personal page may run potential clients off. Sprinkle them in along with family photos, inspiration, funny post, etc.. This way people won't feel as if all you're trying to do is sell something.

Summary

I was inspired to write this book because I know how difficult it can be as a direct sales leader. I will never forget before joining Avon that a family member advised me not to join any direct sales company. Of course with the determination that I've always had not trying wasn't an option. I knew going in that it would be hard but had nothing to lose. I was always the shy person afraid to talk to strangers let a lone tell them about my new business. I learned quickly that if I wanted my business to grow that I would have to do what it takes to make it happen. Direct sales is not an eight to five but should be treated like a real career. It's easy to get spoiled especially if direct sales is a person's only career. Staying in the bed everyday for long hours not being productive is not the thing to do.

The great thing about direct sales is that I can work in my pajamas as long as I am consistently putting forth some effort. It takes time to build any business and we all go through those ups and downs. The truth is that we don't have to be afraid of being successful. It's great to know that we can earn as much or as little as we want. With the flexibility of being a direct sales leader, business owners can earn extra money for kids college or for any future goals. We can even quit our day job if we want. The possibilities are endless but we must put forth every effort to find out how to be successful.

Join any of my teams!

Avon

www.youravon.com/vsheffield

CareDP

Become a Broker—Free Signup

www.caredpbroker.com/new-agent/

Get Dental Discounts

www.vsheffield.caredp.com

Victoria Collection

Fashion Jewelry & Accessories

www.viccollection.com

Email Me If You're Interested In

Coaching Sessions or to Learn About Other Books or Special Trainings

sheffieldvictoria39@gmail.com

www.ingramcontent.com/pod-product-compliance
Lightning Source LLC
Chambersburg PA
CBHW082242220526
45469CB00012B/2844